MODERN PUBLISHING'S UNAUTHORIZED

WHO'S WHO
OF
BEVERLY HILLS,
9 0 2 1 0

BY
SHARON J. GINTZLER

Modern Publishing
A Division of Unisystems, Inc.
New York, New York 10022

Printed in the U.S.A.

Front and Back Cover Photos: © Fox Broadcasting Company

Cover and Interior Book Design by: Bob Feldgus

Book Number: 10635
ISBN Number: 1-56144-145-7

CONTENTS PAGE

Kicking back and enjoying the spotlight, the cast of *Beverly Hills, 90210* is tickled pink to be tops among TV viewers.
© Fox Broadcasting Company

INTRODUCTION

Just what *is* it about *Beverly Hills, 90210* that makes it one of *the* most popular television shows *ever,* so much so that although its focus is mainly on a group of teens attending fictional West Beverly Hills High, it appeals to "kids" of all ages—say from eight to eighty?

Beverly Hills, 90210 is the kind of show that makes you want to finish your homework extra early so that you can tune in at 9:00 sharp every Thursday night. It makes you say to your friends (and vice versa): "Make sure *not* to call me between nine and ten tonight, okay?!" 'Cause you don't want *any* interruptions at that important time. And it makes you want to get to school extra early on Friday morning so you can talk to your friends all about last night's incredible episode. And—not only doesn't your mom not mind you watching, she actually enjoys watching it *with* you!

Well, the appeal and magic of *BH, 90210* certainly has to do with the fact that it's probably the first show in TV history that deals realistically with the lives, souls and innermost feelings of teenagers. It takes teens *seriously.* The approach to the trials and tribulations, good times and tough times of being a teen today is handled in a truthful and honest manner. As one young viewer expresses: "It's about things that *really* happen, not the stupid things they usually have on TV shows about teenagers."

As all fans know, *90210* centers around the Walsh family, mom, dad and teenage twins Brandon and Brenda, who moved from the midwest (Minneapolis) to Beverly Hills. It's about how "Bran" and "Bren" adjust to their new lives, which include a whole new circle of friends.

The show, which first aired in fall 1990, has gained in popularity as time has gone by. Why? Well, beyond the terrific and believable plotlines of this highly rated series lies another important reason for this show's super success, and that is the highly talented ensemble of young actors who breathe life into the main teen characters. Namely, Luke Perry (brooding and mysterious rich kid Dylan McKay), Jason Priestley (good natured, level-headed Brandon Walsh), Shannen Doherty (his outspoken twin sister Brenda), Tori Spelling (rich girl Donna Martin), Ian Ziering (rich jock Steve Sanders), Brian Austin Green (sort of nerdy, younger guy David Silver), Jennie Garth (rich, blonde and beautiful Kelly Taylor) and last, but certainly not least, Gabrielle Carteris (brainy gal from wrong side of the tracks Andrea Zuckerman).

These eight young actors have no doubt helped make *Beverly Hills, 90210* the hit series that it is today. Virtual "nobodys" not that long ago, all these stars, to one degree or another,

Beverly Hills here we come! The Walshes make their move and TV history, too! *Left to right:* Shannen Doherty, Carol Potter, James Eckhouse, Jason Priestley. © Fox Broadcasting Company

suddenly find themselves in the celebrity spotlight. Newspapers, magazines and TV shows want to photograph and interview them, and fans can't get enough of them!

But—just how *did* these guys and gals get to the enviable position they are in today? And just *who* are they, anyway? In the pages to follow, you'll not only find the answers to the above questions, but tons of facts and probably anything you'll *ever* need to know about the *90210* kids.

That said... happy reading!

There's no denying Luke's star appeal—he receives 3,000 fan letters a week and is mobbed at malls! © Fox Broadcasting Company

CHAPTER 1

LUKE'S PLEASIN' TOP-TO-TOE FACT FILE

Full Name: **Coy Luther Perry III**
Birthdate: **October 11 (He wants to keep the year a secret.)**
Birthplace: **Mansfield, Ohio**
Grew Up In: **Fredericktown, Ohio**
Current Residence: **Hollywood, California**
Height: **5'10"**
Weight: **150 pounds**
Hair Color: **Brown**
Eye Color: **Brown**
Pet: **Jerry Lee, his pot-bellied pig**
Favorite Musician: **Jerry Lee Lewis**
Favorite Actors & Actresses: **Marlon Brando, James Woods, Tommy Lee Jones, Ed Harris, Pamela Reed, Annie Potts**
Favorite Movies: ***Cool Hand Luke, The Abyss, The Pope of Greenwich Village***
Favorite TV Shows: ***S.W.A.T., Starsky & Hutch, Married: With Children***
Favorite Food: **Steak**
Favorite Drink: **"H$_2$O"**
His Least Favorite Feature About Himself: **"My skinny legs!"**
Latest Project: **Just signed a two-picture deal with 20th Century Fox Films.**

LUKE PERRY: SMALL-TOWN BOY FINDS FAME AND FORTUNE

"I love where I come from," states Ohio-born-and-bred Luke Perry, who hasn't forgotten his small-town, down-home roots, even though he has skyrocketed to fame and fortune virtually overnight starring as Dylan McKay on the hot television show *Beverly Hills, 90210.* As Dylan, rich guy with a heart of gold and sensitivity to spare, this handsome actor has certainly discovered superstardom!

Luke was raised in the tiny farming town of Fredericktown (population 2,300), an hour's drive from Columbus. His parents divorced when Luke was just a small lad of six, and Luke says that he was never close to his birth-dad. In fact, he's always been extremely close to the man his mom, Ann, remarried when Luke was twelve, construction worker Steve Bennett. Says the brown-eyed star: "He's the greatest man I know. I love him... He's the one who taught me the important things I needed to know about being a man." Truth be told, "Hollywood Star" Luke is incredibly close to his entire family, including his mom, stepdad, brother (Tom, 28, a Navy recruiter), sister (Amy, 22, a secretary), and stepsister (Emily, 15).

You may find it hard to believe, but Luke

A match made in heaven—Brenda and Dylan 4-ever!

actually remembers wanting to be an actor ever
since the age of five! He vividly remembers
lying in bed one night, listening to the TV set
as his mom watched the movie *Cool Hand
Luke*, starring Paul Newman. Well, *our*
favorite Luke kept hearing his own name
mentioned over and over again, and that
caught his attention. Later on, when he found
out that Paul Newman was from Ohio, Luke
decided to try acting, too.

As a youngster, Luke would sing and dance
and do impressions, and finally in high school
he tried to seek out ways to pursue his acting
ambitions. As one story goes, he was kicked
out of a school production. But there was

also the time Luke got to "spread his wings" as his school's mascot, "Freddie Bird," when he dressed himself in a funny outfit consisting of yellow tights and red feathers, among other things, and had himself airlifted by helicopter right into the middle of a football game!

The fact was, although he was voted Biggest Flirt in his high school yearbook and got to participate in sports like baseball, the acting bug had bitten Luke hard. He realized that in order to seriously pursue his dream of becoming an actor, he'd have to leave the limitations of his hometown behind him and follow his dream to Hollywood. "I had big ambitions," this soft-spoken fellow recalls, "and living in a small town and not being able to do anything

Luke's a small-town boy with big city ambitions. Jeff Mayer/Star File Photos

about my goals was very frustrating." So, right after he graduated from Fredericktown High School, Luke packed his bags and moved to Los Angeles to study his chosen craft.

Luke earned money for acting classes by doing all kinds of odd jobs like laying asphalt and working in a doorknob factory! He appeared in commercials and did some stage work, all the while auditioning for bigger and better roles. Then, finally, at audition number 217 (he was counting!) he landed the part of Ned Bates on the ABC-TV afternoon soap opera *Loving,* for which he relocated to New York in 1987. Luke appeared on that show for one year, and for the next two years he remained in New York doing commercials for products like Levi's 501 jeans and appearing briefly in the soap opera *Another World.* (He played Kenny.) Then, in 1990, Luke returned to Los Angeles and won the role that would make him a household name: that of Dylan McKay on *90210,* of course!

When Luke auditioned for the role of Dylan the producers knew they had found the actor they'd been searching for. Luke was handsome, soft-spoken and mysterious. Luke "was excited" about playing Dylan because he felt the character had a lot of depth to him.

Which is what also can be said about Luke himself!

Jason's fabulous face of the 90s makes fans swoon.
© Sunny Bak/Shooting Star

CHAPTER 2
JASON'S PRIVATE FACT FILE

Full Name: **Jason Bradford Priestley**
Birthdate: **August 28, 1969**
Birthplace: **Vancouver, British Columbia (Canada)**
Current Residence: **Woodland Hills, California**
Height: **5′8″**
Weight: **140 pounds**
Hair Color: **Dark blond/light brown (However you choose to look at it!)**
Eye Color: **Blue-green**
Résumé: *Sister Kate, 21 Jump Street, MacGyver, Quantum Leap,* **Disney Channel TV movies** *Teen Angel & Teen Angel Returns*
Favorite Authors: **Jack Kerouac, Ian Fleming, Robert Ludlum**
Fave Foods: **Mexican & Chinese**
Future Goal: **To direct**
Fave Sports: **Hockey, golf, snow skiing, tennis, rugby, sailing**
Fave Actors: **Robert Duvall, Al Pacino, James Woods**
Fave Transportation: **He presently drives a Yamaha motorcycle!**
Fave date: **Going to the movies.**

JASON PRIESTLEY: BABY, LOOK AT HIM NOW

It wouldn't be that much of an exaggeration to say that Jason Priestley was *born* to act! After all, his adorable face first appeared on the screen when he was a tiny baby—playing the part of a crying infant in a commercial. He was recommended for the part by his mom, who just happened to be the actress holding him in his public debut! And it's been pretty much smooth sailing from there for this Vancouver, British Columbia-born guy, who's presently starring as Brandon Walsh on *Beverly Hills, 90210.*

But let's go back a few years. You might say that this August 28, 1969-born doll's career really started at the still-tender age of four, when he was convinced that he could do what he saw other children doing on TV. He actually begged his mom, Sharon, a former dancer-actress-choreographer-singer, to take him to her agent—and Jason was signed almost immediately!

He started by working in local commercials in his native Canada. By the age of eight, he had starred in his first made-for-television movie, *Stacey,* for the CBC (Canadian Broadcasting Corporation). Says Jason: "I did a lot of commercials in Canada until I was eleven or twelve. Then I sort of dropped out of it. I was

On the set, Jason wows fans like no other heartthrob can!
Mark Weiss/MWA

playing a lot of hockey and rugby. But then, at about fourteen, I decided that I wanted to go back into acting because I really enjoyed it. I started training and studying and I jumped back in...."

He also got himself a manager who was based in Los Angeles, and Jason appeared in many different TV series like *21 Jump Street, Quantum Leap, MacGyver* and *Airwolf;* TV movies like *Lies From Lotus Land* and *Nobody's Child;* feature films like *Watchers, The Boy Who Could Fly* and *Nowhere To Run,* and stage productions like *The Breakfast Club,*

Rebel Without A Cause and *Addict.* In order to do all of this work Jason found himself jetting back and forth between Canada and L.A., for about a year. Then, in 1987, after he graduated from high school, Jason finally decided to make a permanent move to Los Angeles because that was where there was work.

That move certainly paid off because in 1989 Jason landed a starring role on a sitcom, *Sister Kate,* in which he played orphan Todd Mahaffey. Though that series was short-lived, it certainly got Jason Priestley noticed by a lot of Hollywood big shots!

.... Including, of course, Aaron Spelling, the producer behind *BH, 90210.* (Actually, according to legend, J's co-star Tori Spelling, who is also Aaron's daughter, saw Jason on *Sister Kate,* thought he was totally cute, and suggested Mr. Priestley for a new series about teens that her dad was casting—*90210,* of course!) In any case, the role of Brandon Walsh was Jason's in the fall of 1990!

How does Jason explain his amazing show biz success? "I think ambition and drive have a lot to do with it," he reflects. "If you stick it out and if you can keep working—take the disappointment and the rejection and keep going and keep your focus and drive—then I think you can rise above it."

He's done TV, movies and stage—does he prefer anything in particular? "I think each one contains a lot of things which I really enjoy. I don't think it's a question of which one I like better—I love them all! It's just that they're different." He enjoys playing Brandon on *90210,* who he describes as "a normal guy thrust into the seemingly glamorous fast-paced Beverly Hills lifestyle, but he's secure enough with who he is not to let go of his midwestern values and morals."

The latest exciting thing that's happening with Jason Priestley is the fact that he's very close to reaching two separate deals with Columbia Pictures, one which would have him star in a movie produced by Penny Marshall, called *Me & Monroe,* the second, which is called in show biz lingo a "first-look deal," that would give Columbia Pictures the rights to any movie Jason wants to produce, direct or star in that is not set up in another studio.

Whew! That's pretty heady stuff for a 22-year-old guy. But then, it seems like Jason Priestley was destined for pretty incredible things!

Shannen's been climbing the superstar stairway since she was ten
years old. Barry King/Gamma Liaison

CHAPTER 3

SHANNEN'S STATS TO THE MAX

Full Name: **Shannen Doherty**
Birthdate: **April 12, 1971**
Birthplace: **Memphis, Tennessee**
Current Residence: **Los Angeles, California**
Height: **5'3"**
Weight: **approximately 100 pounds**
Hair Color: **Dark brown**
Eye Color: **Hazel**
Family: **Dad, Tom; Mom, Rosa; Older Brother, Sam**
Résumé: ***21 Jump Street, Life Goes On, Magnum, P.I., The Outlaws, Airwolf, The Voyagers, The Other Lover* with Lindsay Wagner and Jack Scalia, miniseries *Robert Kennedy and His Times* with Brad Davis and Jack Warden**
Hobbies: **Reading, tennis, snow skiing, exercising and especially horseback riding**
Pets: **3 dogs and 3 doves**
Best Friends on *90210:* **She's closest to Jason Priestley and Tori Spelling**
Biggest Fear: **"Horror films!"**

THE SECRETS OF SHANNEN DOHERTY'S SUCCESS

This spunky gal—who portrays to perfection Brandon's twin sister Brenda Walsh on *90210* (who dates Dylan!)—has always been driven and determined to succeed!

Twenty-year-old Shannen, who was born on April 12, 1971 to Rosa and Tom Doherty in Memphis, Tennessee, and who has an older brother, knew at an early age that she wanted to act. One thing that probably affected this decision was her family's move to Los Angeles— the Land of Entertainment—when Shannen was just six years old. She discovered she loved acting by chance, when she accompanied a friend to an audition. Recalls this dark-haired, hazel-eyed beauty: "When I was eight and a half, a friend invited me to watch the audition for a children's theatre production of *Snow White.* The director invited me to audition and, after some prodding, I finally did. Boy—was I surprised when I landed one of the lead parts!" Shannen played the dwarf "Sneezy" in the production, and from that moment on she was hooked on acting!

When Shannen tried to persuade her parents to let her stick with it, Rosa and Tom were reluctant. So, Shannen was determined to

Girl in the middle, Shannen, rounds out the ravishing trio of cliquers on *Beverly Hills, 90210*. © Fox Broadcasting Company

prove to them that she was *really* serious. For about the next two years she hung around the theatre, trying to soak up as much knowledge as possible about her chosen craft, like learning how to do makeup and even sweeping the stage! When her folks realized that their driven daughter was really willing to give it her all, they finally were convinced that Shannen was serious and she signed on with an agent.

Shannen impressed many casting agents with her natural talent and started working professionally almost immediately. Her first professional role was at age ten in the animated movie *Secret of NIMH* (she was the voice of Teresa). Then this 5'3" bundle of energy guest-starred on such shows as *Superkids, Magnum P.I., The Voyagers, Life Goes On* and *21 Jump Street,* before her really big break came in 1981. The late actor Michael Landon, who had seen some of her performances, was so impressed with Shannen's talent that he gave her the role of Drucilla on his series *Father Murphy.* He then cast her in two more of his series, *Little House: A New Beginning* and *Highway to Heaven.* (Landon was *so* taken with Shannen's performance as Jenny Wilder in *Little House* that he created a few episodes of the show especially for her character!) "I loved working with Michael Landon," the petite actress recalls somewhat wistfully. "We really felt like a family." (When Shannen learned of Landon's death from cancer in July '91 she locked herself in her *90210* dressing room and cried her eyes out. He had been an important person in her life—her friend, teacher, professional advisor and supporter, a tower of strength.)

After she left *Little House* Shannen had a ton of guest-starring roles on TV, appeared in the movie *Girls Just Want to Have Fun* (based on the Cyndi Lauper song) and was then cast as Kris Witherspoon on the series *Our House.* She reveals that her experience on this show made her realize just how tough was the reality of

Shannen fondly remembers working with the late, great Michael Landon in *Little House: A New Beginning*. © Bob Villard/Access Archive

show biz. "A lot of girls think [acting] is all parties," Shannen said at the time, when she was about 15, "but most of the time I'm too tired to party!"

Following her role on *Our House,* Shannen starred in the movie *Heathers.* When she was asked which she preferred, acting in movies or on television, she enthused: "I enjoy all aspects of acting and I'm happy with the opportunities I've had."

When she was cast as Brenda Walsh in 1990 for the new series about teens, *Beverly Hills, 90210,* it was like a dream-come-true for Shannen—and she plunged into the role enthusiastically. She loves the realism with which *90210* portrays being a teenager. "I have no interest in being on a show that makes young adults look like they have no brains... no values or morals," she says. "I have no interest in shows like that."

And Shannen feels a lot of responsibility toward her fans now that she's become a teen role model. "I can't go anywhere without somebody recognizing me," she says. "There are thousands of Brenda imitators out there ... Brenda is a positive role model, but not a perfect one ... she learns from her mistakes, and so do I."

These days Shannen says she's extra happy because she has a new man in her life, Chicago businessman Chris Foufas, who reportedly gave her a 6½-carat diamond ring! They have plans to marry in the near future. As for her "reel" life romance with Dylan (Luke Perry) on *90210,* this outspoken gal reveals that if she could pick one of her co-stars as a real life date, it would be ... Jason Priestley!

Playing bad boy Steve Sanders is a challenge for good guy Ian Ziering.
Movie Star News

CHAPTER 4

IAN'S PERSONAL DATA SHEET

Full Name: **Ian Andrew Ziering**
Birthdate: **March 30 (year unknown)**
Birthplace: **West Orange, New Jersey**
Current Residence: **Los Angeles, California**
Height: **6'**
Weight: **175 pounds**
Hair Color: **Blond**
Eye Color: **Blue**
Family: **Mom, Mickie; Dad, Paul; and two
  older brothers, Jeffrey and Barry**
Pets: **Coty, a dog, and salt-water fish in a
  huge 55-gallon tank**
Résumé: *Guiding Light, Love Of Life* **and**
  The Doctors. **He also had the lead in**
  Flour Babies, **an afterschool special,
  and made his motion picture debut in**
  Endless Love **starring Brooke Shields. Ian's
  also done theater including** *I Remember
  Mama* **on Broadway and the national
  tour of** *Peter Pan.*
Hobbies: **"Keeping salt-water fish."**
Little Known Fact About Him: **For two years,
  Ian was the voice of the boy on the Lucky
  Charms commercials!**

IAN ZIERING:
NOT REALLY A BAD BOY
AT ALL

When Ian (pronounced EYE-an) Ziering was growing up in West Orange, New Jersey—just a stone's throw away from the bright lights of New York City's Broadway—he always dreamed of performing on stage. From early on he loved watching musicals and listening to their lyrics. He loved them so much in fact, that the young Ian would croon show tunes in the shower! His favorites? "You know, the old stuff," he says. "I loved Rodgers and Hammerstein best of all."

His talent proved itself early on and he quickly earned parts in elementary school productions. "In fourth grade I played George M. Cohan in a school show and I played Doody in *Grease* in a camp production," recalls Ian of his earliest performing days. "But, hey, that stuff was small potatoes. I thought that was as close as I'd get to being a star." Too bad he didn't have a crystal ball....

Following the "small potatoes" school productions, he soon began auditioning for roles on Broadway. A producer recognized Ian's acting and singing talents and cast him as the understudy in a production of *I Remember Mama*.

"I thought, 'Great. I'm an understudy. With my luck the kid who's got the role will never miss a day!'" But, as luck would have it, the actor Ian was understudying had to miss a performance and Ian stepped in!

"I was a total nervous wreck," Ian remembers. But, despite his jitters and butterflies, Ian went on with the show, giving the best performance he knew how to give. The producers were so impressed, they hired him to take over the role permanently!

Ian continued to win roles in community theater and commercials and by the time he was 12 years old, he'd auditioned for and won the role of Brooke Shields' brother in the feature film *Endless Love*. And though theater

Taking a break with man's best friend, Ian shares the spotlight with his dog, Coty. © Mark Weiss/MWA

Taking time out between takes for a bear hug, Ian and Gabrielle share a special moment before getting back to work. © Mark Weiss/MWA

was and always will be Ian's first love, it was through TV that he really started to make it.

Before *90210* was even an idea in the producer's head, Ian was gaining experience on the daytime soap operas. Prior to playing Steve Sanders, *90210*'s resident bad boy, Ian's biggest role had been his two-year stint as Cameron Stewart on the daytime drama *Guiding Light.* Other recurring roles included parts on such serials as *Love Of Life* and *The Doctors.* He also nabbed the lead role in *Flour Babies,* a critically-acclaimed afterschool special directed by actress Linda Lavin.

When Ian headed out to California a few years later to audition for his current *90210* role, he felt a little uneasy about working in Hollywood, even though he had more than a few terrific credits under his belt. He sought the role of spoiled, rich kid Steve and played it like he was acting out his own life, though his own childhood experiences had been so vastly different from Steve's. Ian's family was just your average middle class suburban clan, unlike Steve's ultra-rich, ultra-famous upbringing.

Perhaps Ian was such a determined young performer because of his dyslexia, a learning disability. "It put a great damper on my academics, so I focused on creative things," he says of overcoming the limits of his condition.

Like his co-stars, Ian is thoroughly relishing his work on *90210*. That his character is evolving to be more likeable suits Ian. He looks forward to the public appearances, especially the ones at high schools across the country where he can hook up one-on-one with kids. "If I can help someone from turning in the wrong direction, then I feel good," says Ian.

When this thoughtful star isn't working on the show or making the publicity rounds, he frequently flies home to visit his family in New Jersey. "There's nothing like going home," smiles Ian.

Jennie Garth may be a newcomer to acting but she is definitely going places. © Fox Broadcasting Company

CHAPTER 5

THE JUICE ON JENNIE

Full Name: **Jennifer Eva Garth**
Birthdate: **April 3, 1972**
Birthplace: **Champaign-Urbana, Illinois**
Current Residence: **Sherman Oaks, California**
Height: **5'5"**
Weight: **112 pounds**
Hair Color: **Blonde**
Eye Color: **Blue**
Family: **Mom, Carolyn; Dad, John; sisters Lisa, Cammie, Wendy and Lynn, and brothers Johnny and Chuck**
Pet: **Sasha, a white poodle**
Résumé: *Brand New Life, Circus Of The Stars, Teen Angel Returns, Just Perfect* **and various TV guest spots including** *Growing Pains.*
First Ambition: **"To be happy and free!"**
Hobbies: **"Playing with my dog and being with my family and friends and dancing!"**

JENNIE GARTH: FARM GIRL AT HEART

On *90210* Jennie Garth plays Kelly Taylor, fictional West Beverly Hills High's slightly snooty, stuck-up, concerned-with-appearances (hers and others), trendy, popular girl. Jennie simply describes Kelly as "a product of her environment." She's got an alcoholic mom and her dad has just disappeared out of her life, and though Jennie is as convincing as can be in her role, her own life story couldn't be more unlike Kelly Taylor's!

Jennie was born in the rural, farming community of Champaign-Urbana, Illinois, where the main campus of the University of Illinois is located. Her parents were farmers who raised Tennessee Walking Horses and ran a riding stable, so Jennie spent many of her growing-up years around animals. As a member of her local 4-H Club, she competed in horse shows and competitions. In fact, she began competing when she was only three years old! The love for animals she developed during her early years on the farm stays with Jennie to this day. She's an avid supporter of animal rights and she's devoted to protecting and preserving the environment.

When Jennie was 13, her family moved to Phoenix, Arizona, for her father's health. And though you could say that Jennie had a history of performing, what with all the horse shows and fairs, it was in Arizona that this young lady was formally introduced to the world of entertaining.

In order to fit into her new environment and make new friends, Jennie enrolled in some dancing classes, and that soon led to participating in local beauty pageants. It was at a state-level competition when she was 16 that Jennie was spotted by Randy James, a Hollywood manager who says he saw something really special in Jennie!

"At first, when he started talking to me, I thought, 'Yeah, sure, right,'" Jennie remembers. "But he talked with my parents and introduced us to his wife and basically said that he thought I had potential."

At her manager's urging, Jennie enrolled in some acting classes and, unbelievably, six months later Jennie and her mom moved to Los Angeles to further pursue Jennie's budding acting career! "My father stayed behind in Phoenix and my mother and I showed up on my manager's doorstep! I think he was amazed that we'd just pulled up our roots and taken off," Jennie laughs!

Like most young up-and-comers in Hollywood, Jennie went on daily auditions (sometimes three or four in a single day!), and remarkably landed her first job, starring opposite Barbara Eden in NBC's *Brand New Life,* after only *four* months in the business! "That was the good news," explains Jennie. "The bad news was that they put us on against *60 Minutes* and we only lasted six episodes!"

Not one to be easily daunted, Jennie hit the audition trail once again and did two films for The Disney Channel, *Teen Angel Returns* (opposite her current co-star Jason Priestley!) and *Just Perfect.* Jennie also learned to fly on trapeze for an edition of *Circus Of The Stars* and did some guest TV spots including one on the hit show *Growing Pains.*

Then *90210* came along and something told Jennie to turn down other work while she waited to hear from the show's producers. Jennie's little voice was right! She got the part of Kelly Taylor after only five auditions! An impressive accomplishment for a relative newcomer to the acting business, to say the least.

Jennie really enjoys working on *90210* and says that the show "is taking on important issues that teens can relate to. I think it's one of the best things on TV now." Now that the show is tops with teens all over the country, Jennie is being recognized more and more. Though sometimes she finds all that fame and recognition a little overwhelming, she wouldn't trade it for the world. "I'm proud to be on this show," Jennie confides. "It teaches kids that it's

Jennie and Jason on the set of *Beverly Hills, 90210* and getting ready for another great performance. © Mark Weiss/MWA

okay to make mistakes and you don't have to grow up too quickly."

Jennie herself has grown up a lot since she's come to Los Angeles. Once she got settled with the show, her mom moved back to Phoenix and Jennie couldn't be more thankful to her wonderful parents for their undying support.

"I can't tell you how great my parents have been," smiles Jennie. "I think my mom will always be a big part of my career," says Jennie. "As long as I'm acting, I would not want to do it without her support."

In real life and "reel" life Brian Austin Green is busting moves and getting his character noticed! Ron Wolfson/London Features International

CHAPTER 6

TOP-TO-TOE BRIAN

Full Name: **Brian Austin Green**
Birthdate: **July 15, 1973**
Birthplace: **Los Angeles, California**
Current Residence: **Los Angeles, California**
Height: **5'7"**
Weight: **135 pounds**
Hair Color: **Light brown**
Eye Color: **Blue**
Family: **Mom, Joyce; Dad, George; older brother, Keith; and older sister, Lori.**
Pets: **Tiko, a dog, and Fluffy, a cat**
Résumé: *Knots Landing.* **He also guested on such series as** *Highway To Heaven, Small Wonder, Fathers and Sons,* **and the TV movies** *The Canterville Ghost, Good Morning Miss Bliss, Choices* **and** *Baby M.* **He also has two feature films to his credit,** *An American Summer* **and** *The Kid.*
Hobbies: **"Working with my music group, 'Think Twice.'"**
Biggest Like: **Girls**
Biggest Dislike: **Liver**

BRIAN AUSTIN GREEN: TYPICAL TEEN

Brian Austin Green plays *90210*'s resident geeky freshman David Silver. In real life, Brian desperately hopes he isn't quite as nerdy as the character he portrays. Born and raised in the Los Angeles area by his professional drummer dad, George, and mom, Joyce, Brian first thought he'd follow in his father's footsteps. Young Brian loved spending time with his dad and "schmoozing" with musician types. But things took a turn toward acting when at the age of 11 he was approached by a University of Southern California graduate film student to star in a class project flick. All it took was that one experience in front of the camera and Brian was hooked! "I was bitten by the acting bug," laughs Brian.

He immediately begged his parents to let him act, and soon started appearing in TV commercials, eventually joining the cast of the top-rated CBS-TV nighttime soap opera *Knots Landing,* playing Donna Mills' son Brian Cunningham. Though he enjoyed the four years he spent on *Knots,* Brian was eager to portray other roles and further pursue his first love—music. While appearing in *Knots Landing,* between regular school, set school and his busy shooting schedule, Brian actually

Brian's chillin' as he plays air hockey at home—a fave pastime.
© Mark Weiss/MWA

found time to continue to audition for roles in other TV and movie projects.

Aside from guest-starring roles in TV series such as *Highway To Heaven, The New Leave It To Beaver, Small Wonder, Fathers And Sons* and *Baywatch,* Brian has also appeared in the TV miniseries *Baby M* and the big screen motion pictures *An American Summer, The Kid* and *Kickboxer II.*

When the opportunity to audition for *90210* arrived, Brian was dead set on winning the role of David Silver, but he found himself competing against his old friend Douglas Emerson, who eventually won the role of Scott Scott and has since been written off the series as the only principal character to have died.

Brian is the first to admit that there are similarities and major differences between himself and the character he portrays. First off, Brian's family life is vastly different from that of his "reel" life persona. "My parents are still together and I have an older brother and sister," explains Brian, who also happens to be older than David.

When you come right down to it, though,

Brian takes a break between takes on the set. © Bob Villard/Access Archive

Brian is just as fun-loving, music-loving and girl-crazy as Mr. Silver. "I don't have a girlfriend," confides Brian, "but I'm looking for one!" The girl of Brian's dreams will hopefully share some of his interests.

In addition to working out and participating in his fave sports which include golfing, surfing, basketball, snow skiing and bicycling, Brian is currently a member of Think Twice, a rap group he started with a few close friends including Robin Thicke, the son of Alan Thicke of *Growing Pains* fame.

"The cast and crew have been really supportive about giving me a chance to show off my talent," says Brian. "I mean, I can remember dancing at the cast party when one of the producers said, 'Hey! We didn't know you could dance!' Next thing I know, I'm busting some moves on the show. They really let me bring a lot of myself to my character." They certainly do! David Silver may be geeky, but he's unquestionably West Beverly Hills High's best dancer! And that's not all! Think Twice was given the chance to perform on an episode of *90210,* and though he was admittedly nervous performing in front of, and not with, his co-stars, once the music was cranked up, Brian got right into it.

Brian sums up his feelings about the many aspects of his career. "I *love* performing!" he states emphatically.

Tori Spelling casts a cool look and plays the role of Donna Martin to perfection. © Fox Broadcasting Company

CHAPTER 7

ALL THE FACTS ON TORI

Full Name: **Victoria Davey Spelling**
Birthdate: **May 16, 1973**
Birthplace: **Los Angeles, California**
Current Residence: **Los Angeles, California**
Height: **5′5″**
Weight: **100 pounds**
Hair Color: **Blonde**
Eye Color: **Brown**
Family: **Mom, Candy; Dad, Aaron; younger brother, Randy.**
Pets: **four dogs: Muffin, Pepper, Shelly and Tiffany**
Résumé: *Saved By The Bell, Monsters, Hotel, The Wizard, The Love Boat, T.J. Hooker, Fantasy Island* **and** *Vegas.* **She also appeared in the TV movie** *The Three Kings* **and the feature film** *Troop Beverly Hills.*
Hobbies: **Shopping, reading and sketching**
Personal Style: **Casual**

TORI SPELLING:
REAL LIFE BEVERLY HILLS BABE

Of all the stars of *Beverly Hills, 90210* Tori Spelling's real life most resembles that of her character's, Donna Martin, West Beverly Hills High's ultra-cool, clothes-conscious, and very funny hip cliquer.

A native Californian, Tori was born and raised in Bel Air, an even *more* wealthy and exclusive Los Angeles suburb than Beverly Hills. Because her father is Aaron Spelling, TV's most successful and well-known producer (including *90210!*), Tori was raised amidst the TV and movie industries. It wasn't an unusual thing in the Spelling household for well-known celebrities the likes of Linda Evans, Farrah Fawcett and Barbara Stanwyck to just drop by for an informal visit. In fact, it was the latter who actually gave Tori her nickname!

"My real name is Victoria," explains Tori. "My parents wanted to name me Victoria but they thought everyone would call me Vicky and they weren't too crazy about that. My dad was real good friends with Barbara Stanwyck and she said, 'Why don't you call her Tori?' Ever since then I've been Tori!"

Being a creative type himself, Tori's dad

always gave her the opportunity and freedom to explore her own interests and goals. And being exposed to the entertainment industry from so early on really had an effect on Tori—she knew she wanted to act.

"I practically grew up on a set," says Tori. "When I was three years old my dad used to let me sit in a director's chair and watch the stars film. My first part was one line on my dad's show *Vegas*. I did it in one take so everyone on the set started calling me 'One-Take Tori.'"

Since that first experience in front of the camera at the tender age of six, Tori was hooked! "Even though I was pretty young, I really enjoyed the work," she remembers. "I knew that I wanted to continue acting because performing seemed natural to me."

Tori honed her acting skills by taking private classes (for over seven years) and soon began racking up the screen credits. She's appeared in a variety of TV shows including *Saved By The Bell, The Love Boat, T.J. Hooker, Hotel,* and the critically-acclaimed ABC-TV movie *The Three Kings.* Tori's even got one big screen credit—opposite Shelley Long in *Troop Beverly Hills.*

When her dad was casting *90210,* he approached his teenage Beverly Hills high schooler for her opinion of who would be appropriate for the starring roles. In fact, it was Tori who recommended Jason Priestley *and* Shannen Doherty (because she'd admired the

Tori helped super producer dad, Aaron Spelling, make all the right moves casting for *Beverly Hills, 90210.* © Mark Weiss/MWA

actress's work in *Heathers*).

Unbeknownst to her dad, Tori also auditioned for a role in *90210!* She originally tried her hand at Kelly Taylor, the role which eventually went to co-star Jennie Garth, but Tori was cast as Donna Martin, a role which wasn't originally a regular. And though some skeptics might say her role became a regular simply because of who Tori's father is, one look at her acting ability shows proof positive that she earned that "promotion" on her own merits.

Like her co-stars, Tori is having the time of her life starring in *90210* and believes that the show sends the right kind of messages to teens everywhere. "I'm really proud of what I'm doing. It's a lot of work, but I love it," she states.

On those rare occasions when she's not putting in grueling hours on the *90210* set, Tori enjoys spending time with her family, which aside from her dad also includes mom Candy, younger brother Randy and four dogs. When she's got a spare moment or two, she enjoys indulging in her favorite pastimes, which include reading, writing, sketching and watching scary horror movies. The scarier the better!

Determination and focus helped Gabrielle achieve her goal of acting.
© Mark Weiss/MWA

CHAPTER 8

THE GOODS ON GABRIELLE

Full Name: **Gabrielle Carteris**

Birthdate: **January 2 (year unknown)**

Birthplace: **Phoenix, Arizona (Gabrielle's family moved to San Francisco, California when she was only six months old—she grew up in the northern California town.)**

Current Residence: **Los Angeles, California**

Height: **5'1"**

Weight: **108 pounds**

Hair Color: **Light brown**

Eye Color: **Hazel**

Family: **Mom, Marlene and Jim, her twin brother**

Pet: **Lucille "Magilacuty" Ball, a bird of the parrot family**

Résumé: *Another World,* the afterschool specials *Seasonal Differences* and *Just Between Friends.* She's also appeared in *Stella,* an off-Broadway play, and various school productions while attending Sarah Lawrence College.

GABRIELLE CARTERIS: ONE DRIVEN GAL

Like Brenda Walsh, Gabrielle Carteris has a fraternal twin brother. And though Gabby and her brother Jim were born in Phoenix, Arizona, neither twin remembers those days in Arizona at all. Gabby's parents divorced when she and her brother were only six months old. Soon after, mom Marlene moved the family to San Francisco, California, where Gabrielle spent her childhood and her mom opened clothing stores.

Always a "focused child," Gabrielle soon developed an interest in the entertainment business. Everything from dance to acting to pantomime intrigued her! Unfortunately, Gabrielle's interest in entertaining wasn't enough. Told she was too short to dance, she turned her attention to pantomime.

"In junior high, a friend of my mom's was a mime," says Gabrielle, recalling her start in the silent art form. "She was writing a book and she asked me to join in some of their games," she adds. "I just got into it." Then, at the tender age of 14, Gabby left the comfort and security of her Marin County, California, home to tour with the mime troupe all over Europe!

She later returned to London, England, and studied acting at two prestigious acting schools,

Light-hearted Gabrielle dashes toward success.
Christopher Voelker/Shooting Star

the Royal Academy of Dramatic Art and the London Academy of Music and Dramatic Art. Her experiences in London really helped Gabrielle gain a better understanding of her craft and a dedication to succeeding that stayed with her all through her years at Sarah Lawrence College in Westchester, New York, where she studied theatrical acting and psychology, and that remains with her even today.

Rivalry on the set? No way, claims the cast of *Beverly Hills, 90210*.
John Storey/Outline

"I just wanted to be an actress more than anything in the world," smiles Gabrielle! "I think I just moved toward that in my life."

But, despite all of her determination and hard work, the road to a successful acting career was not an easy one for Gabrielle. Unbelievably, she was told she didn't have what it would take to make it in Hollywood.

"It was like, 'Gabrielle, we really like you, but you know, your look is not quite right.' Not what they were looking for—different, odd."

Though this was a harsh ego blow, Gabrielle didn't let it daunt her one bit. Instead, she became even more determined to prove the Hollywood big-wigs wrong.

While in college, she appeared in several critically-acclaimed roles in the regional productions of *Les Liaisons Dangereuses, The Mule And The Milky Way,*and others. And, it was also at this time that Gabrielle became involved in working with deaf people and became a sign language interpreter.

The close proximity of Sarah Lawrence to New York City led to a role in an off-Broadway production and several locally-produced afterschool specials. Then her big break came! The producers of the NBC soap opera *Another World* were so impressed with her work that they created a role just for her!

After a stint on daytime TV, Gabrielle decided it was time to go after roles in primetime and she ventured back to her West Coast roots, only this time headed for Los Angeles. Auditions came quickly and soon she auditioned for *Beverly Hills, 90210,* originally for the role of Brenda Walsh! The usual bunch of callbacks gave Gabby a serious case of nerves, but her fears proved unfounded when she was offered the role of Andrea Zuckerman, the brainy, headstrong, politically active student at West Beverly Hills High.

Gabrielle feels a real bond with Andrea because, as the actress puts it, "we all feel slightly misunderstood." Of her character, she says, "Everything I like about Andrea are things I like about myself. We both have a strong sense of right and wrong." But what about the differences between herself and her TV alter-ego? "She's more conservative. I was a little more out there, I think."

Right now, Gabrielle is as happy as can be playing the role of Andrea. But with a typical day of shooting often lasting sixteen hours plus, this petite actress has little free time on her hands these days. When a spare moment does suddenly become available, you usually won't find Gabrielle hibernating alone. Most likely she'll be using her free time to help other people, whether it's continuing her work with the deaf and hearing-impaired, or volunteering for causes she believes in, like education, The Pediatric AIDS Foundation or Mothers Against

Drunk Driving.

Gabrielle is currently living in the San Fernando Valley, a suburb of Los Angeles. She's happy with her life, which now includes her boyfriend Charlie, who used to be her stockbroker back in her New York days, and her pet conure (a bird of the parrot family).

"I'm very happy with what I'm doing right now," she beams. "I am having the time of my life!"

Gabrielle Carteris is on the right track playing Andrea Zuckerman, the girl from the wrong-side-of-the-tracks on *Beverly Hills, 90210.*
© Mark Weiss/MWA

PHOTO ALBUM

The *Beverly Hills, 90210*
first season cast from
left to right: Ian, Jennie,
Luke, Gabrielle,
Shannen, Doug Emerson,
Jason, Tori and Brian.
© Fox Broadcasting Company

Relaxing at home in a rare moment off, Jason is just an ordinary guy.
Mark Sennet/ Onyx

Jason and Ian monkeying around between takes on the set of *Beverly Hills, 90210*.
© Mark Weiss/ MWA